AMAZING ANCIENTS!

THE ACTIVITY BOOK THAT BRINGS HISTORY TO LIFE

WORLD OF MAYA

PENGUIN WORKSHOP
An Imprint of Penguin Random House LLC, New York

by Elaine A. Kule
illustrated by DGPH Studio

Copyright © 2020 by Penguin Random House LLC. All rights reserved. Published by Penguin Workshop, an imprint of Penguin Random House LLC, New York. PENGUIN and PENGUIN WORKSHOP are trademarks of Penguin Books Ltd, and the W colophon is a registered trademark of Penguin Random House LLC. Manufactured in China.

Visit us online at www.penguinrandomhouse.com.

ISBN 9780593093061   10 9 8 7 6 5 4 3 2 1

MEET THE MAYA

The ancient Maya were one of the earliest civilizations in a historical region called Mesoamerica, which means "middle America." The ancestors of the Maya started traveling from North America about eleven thousand years ago. After many years of wandering from place to place, they settled on lands that are now parts of Mexico and the Central American countries of Guatemala, Belize, Honduras, and El Salvador. The climate is warm. The location has flatlands, called lowlands, where the rainfall can be heavy. The highlands have mountains and areas of rich soil. There are many rivers and dense jungles. There are also sandy coastlines along the Pacific Ocean, the Gulf of Mexico, and the Caribbean Sea.

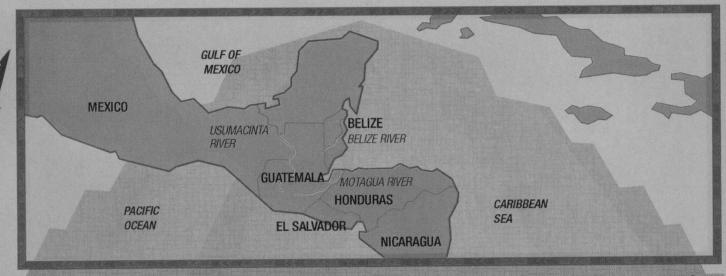

The Maya's history is divided into three main parts. The Preclassic period began around 1800 BCE and lasted until 250 CE. People established villages, many of which developed into city-states, or small kingdoms, led by powerful families. Over time, those families became royal figures. The Classic period lasted from 250 to 900 CE, when the Maya experienced their greatest achievements. The end of the ancient Maya civilization began during what is called the Postclassic period, from 900 to 1524 CE. Historians blame wars, diseases, and a shortage of rainfall that made it impossible to grow crops.

1800 BCE to 250 CE The Preclassic period

250 to 900 CE The Classic period

900 to 1524 CE The Postclassic period

1524 CE The Spanish Conquest of the Maya began

1697 CE The last Postclassic Maya kingdom, Nojpeten, fell to Spain

The Maya hunted and ate deer, duck, and fish. They gathered fruits and other plants in their forests. Many became farmers and settled in the flat lowlands. Corn, also called maize, was their first crop, followed by beans, squash, and chili peppers. Corn, though, became the most important food, not only within the Maya world but throughout Mesoamerica (an area that extends approximately from central Mexico through northern Costa Rica). The Maya boiled the kernels in water mixed with lime, a mineral found in the soil. The process made corn more nutritious because it added vitamins that corn, eaten alone, does not have.

The Maya crushed corn using a hand tool called a mano, similar to a rolling pin. They pressed it against a stone worktop called a metate. The corn flour was then molded into dough. The Maya steamed it in a corn husk and made a food called tamales. Tortillas are thin pancakes made of corn. The Maya toasted them on a clay plate that rested on a hearth, or stone fireplace. Tucked inside the folded tortillas might be meat and vegetables. Because the Maya did not have forks or spoons, they used tortillas to scoop up food.

The Maya also picked pods filled with beans from cacao trees (say: keh-KOW). They boiled, roasted, and then ground the beans to make a chocolate drink mixed with water. They added chili peppers, cornmeal, and sometimes flavorings like cinnamon and vanilla.

CHOCOLATE MILK USING THE MAYA METHOD

The chocolate drinks that the Maya enjoyed were not as sweet as what we drink today. But they liked them bubbly! They poured the liquid back and forth from one cup to another to make it thick and foamy.

FOR AN EASY CHOCOLATE DRINK WITH A SWEETER TASTE, FOLLOW THIS RECIPE:

INGREDIENTS

1 ½ teaspoons unsweetened cocoa powder

1 cup (8 oz.) cold milk

1 teaspoon or less of powdered sugar
(you can always add more)

DIRECTIONS

1. Mix the unsweetened cocoa powder into the cold milk.

2. Add the powdered sugar, and stir.

3. Enjoy it the Maya way by carefully pouring it from one cup into another several times until it's foamy.

MAYA SOCIETY

Kings and queens ruled over Maya society. They gained their titles at birth or through marriage. Because there were different royal families, there was never one united Maya empire.

Religious leaders, called priests, and noblemen made up the next level of Maya civilization. The priests guided religious observances. The nobility advised the rulers. Writers, or scribes, formed the third group. They were among the few people who could read and write. Because the Maya believed that writing was a gift from the gods, they thought scribes were very important people. The next level in society belonged to artists, followed by successful merchants or tradespeople.

The largest group within the Maya population were laborers: the farmers, hunters, fishermen, and builders. Men and older boys performed these jobs. Aside from constructing homes for their families, they built palaces for their rulers. They also constructed pyramids and temples, where religious ceremonies were held.

Soldiers who had been captured during wars between Maya city-states were at the bottom of the Maya world. They, along with anyone who had committed a crime, became slaves.

Women and older girls looked after babies and small children. They worked in their gardens, prepared food, and used looms to weave cotton into cloth to make clothing. They created bowls and pots out of clay. People gathered clay along the riverbanks in the highland areas. They strengthened it with sand or ash, which is found in the remains of fires. Workers also supplied food, clothing, and pottery for royalty, priests, and the upper classes. Farmers grew food for everyone. Royalty and the upper classes had skilled craftspeople produce cloth for their clothing. They also created pottery for them.

People used dried cacao beans as money. They also traded handmade items like weapons. Knives and axes were made from a sharp glass called obsidian—a kind of volcanic rock. Those who lived near the ocean and other waterways produced and exchanged salt. Traders paddled eighty-foot-long canoes to exchange products with different Maya communities and other societies, including the nearby Olmec. Through trade, the exchange of ideas and cultures spread throughout the region.

HOW DID THE MAYA COLLECT SALT?

The Maya sometimes gathered salt by heating seawater in clay pots until the water evaporated and only the salt remained. They also filled shallow pans with seawater and left them out in the hot sun. When the water evaporated, they collected the salt.

WEAVE YOUR OWN PLACE MAT

THE MAYA USED A LOOM TO WEAVE THEIR COTTON CLOTH. BUT YOU CAN WEAVE A PLACE MAT WITH PAPER!

You'll need:
- Two or three pieces of different-colored construction paper
- A ruler
- Scissors
- A pencil
- A glue stick

Follow these simple steps:

1. Position one piece of paper widthwise.

2. Use the ruler to measure about 2 inches from the left side of the paper's edge. With your pencil, draw a vertical line from top to bottom.

3. From the 2-inch line, measure about 1 1/2 inches over and draw another line. Repeat until you reach the edge of the paper.

4. Fold the paper in half vertically (the long way).

5. Cut slits along the horizontal lines, but do not cut to the edge of the paper! Stop cutting when you reach the 2-inch vertical line on the left.

6. Turn the paper over so the pencil marks don't show.

7. Cut 1-inch strips from one of the other colored pieces of paper—or from both if you want more colors on your finished place mat.

8. Weave the strips over and under the cut lines until you reach the end of the paper. Gently pull each strip as far left as you can to close any open spaces.

9. Use the glue stick to secure the tops and bottoms of each strip to the mat.

ENJOY YOUR NEXT MEAL ON YOUR NEW PLACE MAT! TACOS, ANYONE?!

AGRICULTURE IN THE MAYA WORLD

The major crops of the ancient Maya were maize (corn), beans, and squash. Home gardens produced tomatoes, sweet potatoes, chili peppers, and pineapples. Avocados, papaya, and cacao grew on nearby trees. The Maya traded crops such as cotton and cacao with other communities.

Many farmers used a method called slash-and-burn agriculture. They burned all the plants and trees to clear a section of the forest or jungle for growing crops. Ashes from the fires enriched the soil, which produced better plants. After a few years, farmers repeated the process in another location so the trees and jungle plants could grow back.

The Maya tried to make use of as much land as they could to feed the region's growing population. They drained wet, muddy swamps and turned them into farms. They cut fields, or areas of open land, into the sides of forested hills and planted crops there. They built canals, which are waterways dug into the land, so that water could flow from one place to another and help the crops grow. Natural wells called cenotes (say: si-NO-tez) were an additional water source.

WHAT IS A CENOTE?

A cenote is a hollow in the earth formed by the collapse of underground caves. It's filled with fresh, natural water that the Maya used for drinking or bathing. They placed religious offerings in some cenotes. The Maya considered them sacred places.

CAN YOU FIND THE NAMES OF SOME OF THE MOST IMPORTANT FOOD AND FLAVORINGS USED BY THE ANCIENT MAYA?

```
T K Q C A Q Z E G K R Q H S L
Y O I K H G M P O T A T O E S
O C M P D I C Y C C A C A O H
S O V A U V L G A Q U M Z V P
P R K J T M D I U A U X W A R
D N Z J D O P N P B J Y O N G
J Z G N D C E K S E M F L I G
S I U B I R I S I H P Q X L S
Q M W R Y V B N U N G P C L N
U E J S O Z Z D N I X A E A P
A L X G V B W S H A B D D R O
S A V O C A D O Y I M E U B S
H B L U M J Z O O A U O A S Y
Y V U V Z U K N V V Z J N N P
Y K C D N D M I G X I X K N S
```

BEANS
SQUASH
AVOCADO
POTATOES
PUMPKIN
CORN

TOMATOES
CINNAMON
VANILLA
CACAO
CHILI PEPPERS

SPIRIT WORLD

THE MAYA RESPECTED THEIR RULERS, BUT THEY WORSHIPPED THEIR GODS. (THERE WERE OVER ONE HUNDRED OF THEM!) TO THE MAYA, THE GODS CONTROLLED THE UNIVERSE AND THEIR LIVES.

Hun Nal Ye, the maize god, represented life itself. Maya artists imagined him as young, handsome, and wearing a lot of jewelry.

Chak, the god of rain, decided whether harvests were successful or not. There are drawings of him holding a snake, lightning rod, or ax.

The sun god, Kinich Ahau, was important, too. He had a beard and traveled around the sky in the daytime. At night he became the jaguar god and explored the underground. The Maya thought he lived in caves.

The creator god, Itzam, was lord of all gods. With large square eyes he watched over day, night, and the sky. The Maya believed he invented books and writing. His wife was the moon goddess, Ix Chel, who controlled healing.

Two monkey brothers oversaw music, dancing, art, and writing.

A couple of paddler gods rode canoes, the Maya's source of transportation. They are shown as old and toothless. Because they sit on opposite sides of the boat, they may represent opposites, such as day and night.

People felt there was a spiritual connection between their royalty and the gods. Rulers believed that, too. They thought that link made them special. They sometimes wore masks to look like the gods and goddesses.

To the Maya, the universe had three levels—the Upperworld, where the gods lived; the Middleworld, where people lived; and the Underworld, where people traveled after death. They thought that caves, the sea, and cenotes were entrances to the Underworld.

The Maya wanted their pyramids to resemble mountains, which they felt were closer to the sky and therefore closer to the gods.

Eclipses frightened the Maya! They thought they looked as though something was biting into the sun or the moon. They believed solar eclipses were an especially bad sign. Astronomers—scientists who study the stars and planets—recorded when the eclipses occurred to predict when they might happen again.

WHAT IS AN ECLIPSE?

Eclipses of the moon (lunar eclipses) happen when Earth comes between the sun and the moon, blocking all or part of the moon's light.

Eclipses of the sun (solar eclipses) happen when the moon comes between the sun and Earth, blocking all or part of the sun's light.

RULERS GOTTA RULE!

Maya royalty held their most special ceremonies in temples atop pyramids. One of their rituals was bloodletting. Members of the royal family, or a shaman—a priest or healer—would cut themselves, letting blood drip onto paper or cotton. Then they would burn it, letting the smoke rise toward the sky. The Maya believed that blood represents life, so this and other sacrifices were a way of thanking the gods for their survival.

WHAT IS A SHAMAN?

Maya shamans gave spiritual advice and led religious services. They prayed for the sick and tried to cure them with special plants. They still fulfill that role in the modern-day Maya world!

Just like in other ancient societies, the Maya had specific customs for burying the dead. Workers were buried under the floor of their homes. Food and a jade bead were put inside their mouths to ease their journey to the Underworld. Families placed small figures of gods made from clay or wood near the body. They also included items the person may have used while they were alive, such as a tool. The graves of priests sometimes contained books.

Some rulers were buried in graves built into tunnel systems within pyramids. Kings were buried with jade masks covering their faces. Queens wore heavy jade necklaces and jade bracelets.

Jade is a hard stone—harder than steel! It is valuable because it is difficult to find. The ancient Maya mined jade in the highlands of Guatemala, in an area called the Motagua River Valley. The Maya carved and polished jade for royalty and the upper classes, and for trading. Artists placed the stones in masks, necklaces, and headdresses.

There are different blue and green shades of jade, but the Maya liked the apple-green color best. It reminded them of growing plants and the lush jungles where they lived.

TWO OF A KIND!
THERE ARE ACTUALLY TWO KINDS OF JADE: JADEITE AND NEPHRITE.

Jadeite is a harder stone, and it is considered more valuable. Jadeite is mostly found in California, Guatemala, and Japan.

Nephrite can be found throughout the world, including China, the United States, and Canada. Experts say even they can have difficulty telling the two stones apart!

MAKE YOUR OWN JADE BRACELET!

YOU CAN MAKE A JADE-AND-GOLD BRACELET OUT OF PIPE CLEANERS!

You'll need: one yellow pipe cleaner and one green pipe cleaner

Follow these steps:

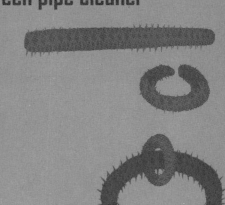

1. Bend the yellow pipe cleaner around your wrist.
2. Twist a green pipe cleaner into a tight circle or spiral, then thread it onto the yellow band. It should look like a green bead.
3. Wrap the ends of the yellow pipe cleaner around each other to form a circle. Leave enough room so you can remove the band easily.
4. Put the bracelet on your wrist. Twist the ends together so that the bracelet fits comfortably. Pull them apart to remove it.

COUNTING YOUR TOES

The Maya created their own number system based on groups of twenty. They began by counting on their ten fingers *and* ten toes. They believed their toes connected them to the earth and wanted to include them! A shell represented *zero,* a pebble equaled *one,* and a stick meant *five.* Over time, the Maya wrote these values using these symbols:

They traded goods using only these three symbols, or glyphs. A glyph is a character used in a writing system to represent a word, number, or sound.

A LITTLE SOMETHING ABOUT NOTHING

The Maya were one of the earliest civilizations to create and use a symbol for zero. They developed it on their own around the year 4 CE, using a placeholder to represent zero.

People who used the placeholder idea before the Maya include the Sumerians and the Babylonians. They lived in what is now the Middle East.

THE CHART BELOW SHOWS THE GLYPHS FOR THE VALUES ZERO THROUGH NINETEEN:

0	1	2	3	4		10	11	12	13	14
5	6	7	8	9		15	16	17	18	19

MAYA MATH!

ALTHOUGH THE ANCIENT MAYA DIDN'T USE SYMBOLS FOR ADDITION AND SUBTRACTION, IT'S EASIER TO COMPLETE THESE EQUATIONS WITH THEM! USE THE CHART TO HELP YOU FILL IN THE VALUE OF EACH GLYPH BELOW AND TO CALCULATE THE ANSWERS.

●●●● + ●●●● = _____

●●●● + ●●●● + ☰ = _____

(••/☰) + •• = _____

(•/☰) – (••••/▬) = _____

●●●● + ▬▬ + (••••/▬) – ●●● = _____

BONUS QUESTION!

To write the numbers twenty through twenty-nine, the Maya used a glyph on the bottom to show how many *ones* there were. A glyph on top showed how many groups of *twenty* there were. The number *twenty* was written like this:

 ⇒ **20**

_____   _____   _____

THE WRITE STUFF!

Scribes created many glyphs to represent the Mayan language. They wrote with brushes made of human hair or stiff animal hair on the inner bark of fig trees. Each page had two columns, read from left to right and from top to bottom, just like a newspaper! Scribes and astronomers recorded information about planets and stars, and also about events within their own culture, in books called codices (say: KO-di-seez). Only four codices still exist.

The *Popol Vuh* is a Maya text that means *Book of the Community*. It includes the creation story of the Maya people. In 1701, a Spanish religious leader decoded it. Over the years, it's been translated into many other languages, including English.

In 1952, language expert Yuri Knorosov realized that some Maya symbols represented sounds, not words. His discovery brought greater understanding to these ancient texts and the glyphs carved into monuments.

THERE ARE OVER EIGHT HUNDRED MAYA GLYPHS.
LEARNING SIX OF THEM IS A GOOD START!
USE THE CHART BELOW TO COMPLETE THE STORY. TRY TO READ THE GLYPHS IN MAYAN!

GLYPH					
WORD IN ENGLISH					
TURTLE	WATER	BOOK	JAGUAR	CROCODILE	SKY
MAYAN WORD					
AK	HA	HUUN	BALAM	AHIN	CHAN

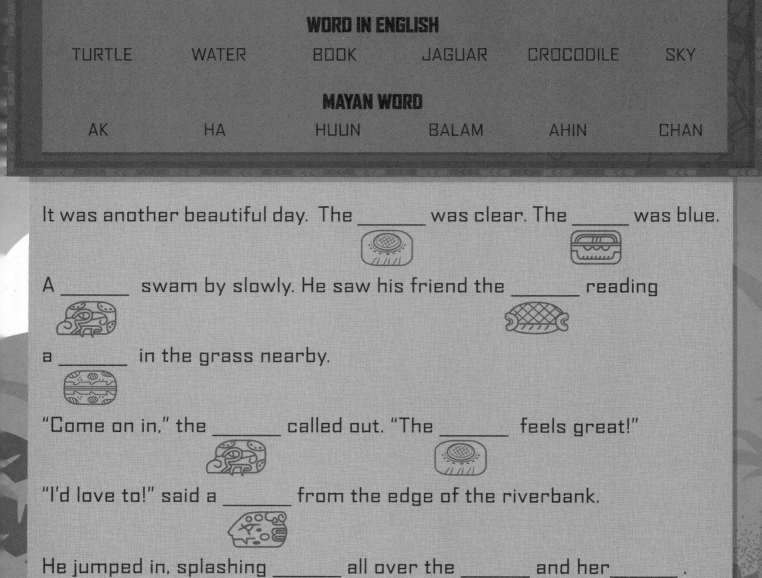

It was another beautiful day. The _____ was clear. The _____ was blue.

A _____ swam by slowly. He saw his friend the _____ reading

a _____ in the grass nearby.

"Come on in," the _____ called out. "The _____ feels great!"

"I'd love to!" said a _____ from the edge of the riverbank.

He jumped in, splashing _____ all over the _____ and her _____ .

"Looks like the _____ came to me!" she said.

LOCATION, LOCATION, LOCATION!

THERE WERE ABOUT FORTY CITY-STATES IN THE MAYA WORLD. THESE WERE THE THRIVING CENTERS OF ROYAL FAMILIES.

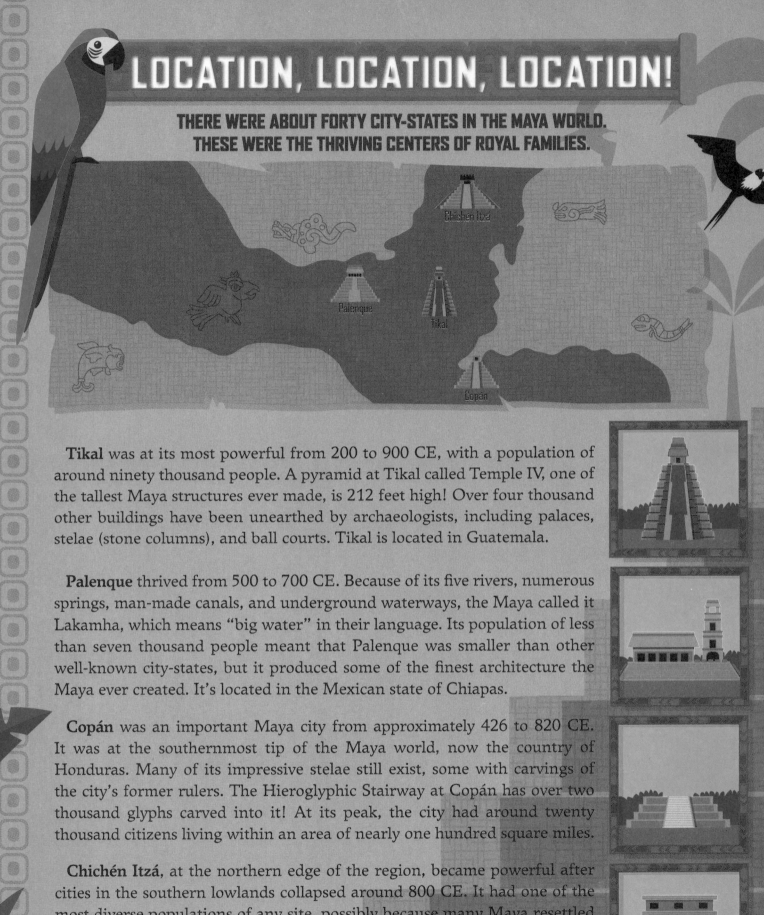

Tikal was at its most powerful from 200 to 900 CE, with a population of around ninety thousand people. A pyramid at Tikal called Temple IV, one of the tallest Maya structures ever made, is 212 feet high! Over four thousand other buildings have been unearthed by archaeologists, including palaces, stelae (stone columns), and ball courts. Tikal is located in Guatemala.

Palenque thrived from 500 to 700 CE. Because of its five rivers, numerous springs, man-made canals, and underground waterways, the Maya called it Lakamha, which means "big water" in their language. Its population of less than seven thousand people meant that Palenque was smaller than other well-known city-states, but it produced some of the finest architecture the Maya ever created. It's located in the Mexican state of Chiapas.

Copán was an important Maya city from approximately 426 to 820 CE. It was at the southernmost tip of the Maya world, now the country of Honduras. Many of its impressive stelae still exist, some with carvings of the city's former rulers. The Hieroglyphic Stairway at Copán has over two thousand glyphs carved into it! At its peak, the city had around twenty thousand citizens living within an area of nearly one hundred square miles.

Chichén Itzá, at the northern edge of the region, became powerful after cities in the southern lowlands collapsed around 800 CE. It had one of the most diverse populations of any site, possibly because many Maya resettled there. Located in the state of Yucatán, Mexico, Chichén Itzá has a ball court that's the largest in the area—nearly double the size of an American football field! It has one of the largest—and most well-known—Maya pyramids, called El Castillo.

HOW WELL DO YOU KNOW THE MOST FAMOUS LOCATIONS IN THE MAYA WORLD?

Down:

1. This site has a stairway with over two thousand glyphs carved into it
3. The name of one of the most famous pyramids in the Maya world
6. Home to one of the tallest Maya pyramids ever constructed

Across:

2. Location of the region's largest ball court
4. A city with many water sources
5. A city or kingdom that governs itself
7. Tikal is located in this country
8. This word means "big water" in the Mayan language

BUILDINGS HERE, THERE, EVERYWHERE!

HOMES

Rulers lived in palaces made of limestone, a hard rock that is common throughout the Maya world. Religious leaders and the nobility lived in large homes on the palace grounds. Scribes, artists, and successful merchants lived in stone houses that were farther away from the city's center. The Maya mostly used stone tools to build those places.

Farmers and other workers lived outside the city. Their houses were made of sticks and dried mud mixed with straw. Thatched roofs made of palm leaves sloped so that rain would drain off. Each home had one door but no windows. Relatives lived close to one another. Their family homes surrounded a central courtyard.

PYRAMIDS AND TEMPLES

Palaces were built close to pyramids. Temples sat on platforms constructed at the top of the pyramids. Maya priests and royalty held ceremonies and prayer services to the gods in the temples. Some of the structures also had watchtowers, where experts believe ancient astronomers watched and recorded the movements of the sun, the moon, planets such as Venus, and solar and lunar eclipses.

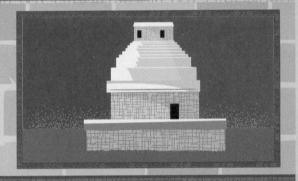

PLAZAS AND STELAE

Plazas were flat, open areas between large buildings. Stelae (say: STEE-lee) are stone columns that were built on the plazas in front of palaces and temples. Each column had important dates about the king and queen carved into them, such as their birthdays and the start of their rule.

BALL COURTS

The Maya built large ball courts made of stone. The size of the courts showed a city-state's power and wealth. The courts had two high walls and stone hoops opposite each other on each wall. There were benches where people could sit and watch the games—much like a modern basketball game! The rules may have been a little more like soccer, though. The goal was to keep the ball in play and score by getting it through the stone hoop. The players could not touch the ball with their hands or feet.

PLAY BALL

The favorite sport of the ancient Maya symbolized a reenactment of the wars between city-states. Warriors who won in battle played against prisoners from the losing side. While the losing team was often killed as a sacrifice, some archaeologists believe that it was the winning team's captain who lost his life!

There were two players or teams in each game. They wore padded clothing for protection. Sometimes they wore fancy headdresses and masks. Each team tried to get the ball—about the size of a soccer ball—through the stone hoops on the arena walls. Ball games were such a big part of Maya life that artists painted scenes of them on murals and pottery and carved them into stone.

RE-CREATE A BALL GAME LIKE THE ONE PLAYED BY THE ANCIENT MAYA

You can play a game similar to the ancient Maya ball game! This is an easy game to play alone or with a friend. You'll need a balloon and a large paper shopping bag. (Headdresses and padding optional!)

BLOW UP THE BALLOON AND KNOT IT ON THE BOTTOM.

HANG ONE HANDLE OF THE SHOPPING BAG ON A DOORKNOB.

TOSS THE BALLOON INTO THE AIR. TRY TO GET IT INTO THE BAG WITHOUT KICKING OR USING YOUR HANDS.

DID YOU KNOW?

The Maya made rubber by draining the sap from rubber trees. They mixed the liquid with an equal amount of juice from morning glory vines. The combination produced balls that really bounced!

Wealthy Maya rulers had staffs of artists working for them full-time. They painted large murals on palaces and temples. They carved pictures and glyphs into stone and wood, and they painted portraits of kings and queens on pottery. They engraved important battle scenes into the wood that framed temple doorways. Jewelry makers crafted jade and shells into ornaments and ceremonial masks.

Both artists and common citizens used clay to make cups, bowls, vases, and small figures of their gods. They created these items for daily use and for trading.

MAKE A MAYA PENCIL HOLDER!

YOU'LL NEED TWO BARS OF MODELING CLAY FOR THIS PROJECT.

1. Mash the bars together and roll them into a ball.

2. Put two fingers in the center of the ball. Move them around to widen the opening.

3. Lift up the sides with your fingers.

4. Flatten the bottom with your hand.

5. Smooth out any bumps or lines.

WITH A PENCIL, CARVE YOUR AGE USING MAYA NUMBER GLYPHS. OR TRY CARVING ONE OF THE ANIMAL GLYPHS SHOWN ON PAGE 15.

TRACKING TIME

Like other groups in the region, the Maya had a system to track the passage of time.

They probably developed their 260-day calendar around 400 BCE. It was divided into thirteen blocks of twenty days, with each day having a name and each block a number. (Kind of like thirteen months with twenty days each.) After the thirteenth block of twenty days passed, the system began again (13 x 20 = 260 days). Some days and numbers predicted good fortune, and others warned of bad luck. People often asked religious leaders to check the calendar for them before doing any important planning.

The Maya also created a 365-day calendar. It had eighteen months, with each month containing twenty days, totaling 360. People throughout the region considered the five extra days to be a frightening period of time. They worried that during those five days, gods of the Underworld could enter the natural world through underground places, such as caves or cenotes, and harm them.

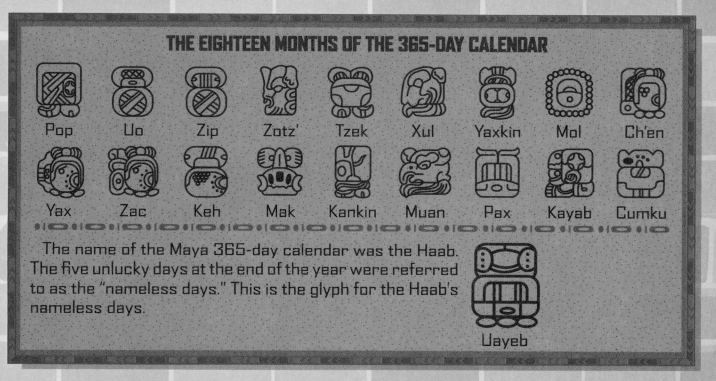

THE EIGHTEEN MONTHS OF THE 365-DAY CALENDAR

Pop   Uo   Zip   Zotz'   Tzek   Xul   Yaxkin   Mol   Ch'en

Yax   Zac   Keh   Mak   Kankin   Muan   Pax   Kayab   Cumku

The name of the Maya 365-day calendar was the Haab. The five unlucky days at the end of the year were referred to as the "nameless days." This is the glyph for the Haab's nameless days.

Uayeb

Centuries later, the Maya developed yet another system known as the Long Count calendar. It marked the passage of time from a day they thought was the first day of the world. They believed this date was August 11, 3114 BCE (according to the modern calendar we use today). The Maya used the Long Count calendar to calculate and carve important dates into their stelae.

The ancient Maya created myths to explain the universe and connect themselves to the gods. They believed that the gods wanted to build people who could think and feel. At first, the gods made figures out of clay. After the clay people melted in the rain, the gods tried wood. But the wooden figures could not think or feel anything. When the gods decided to create humans from corn dough, the beings spoke, and the gods were pleased.

From this story, the Maya believed that the gods made them from corn, which came to symbolize life itself.

In the *Popol Vuh,* a book that contains the Maya creation story, we learn about the brave Hero Twins. Their myth is among the oldest in the Maya culture. The brothers were expert hunters and ball players. Some people believe they represented day and night, or the sun and the moon, or even life and death.

In one story, the twins play a noisy ball game and anger the gods of the Underworld. They challenge the gods to a game and win! In another tale, they destroy an evil bird. There is also a story about the Hero Twins turning their half-brothers into monkeys, who became the gods of music, artwork, and writing.

THE MAYA TREE OF LIFE

A tree of life, or central world tree, is common in many cultures around the world. For the Maya, the tree symbolized the center of the universe. The trunk represents Earth, the roots connect to the Underworld, and the branches uphold the sky. Maya artwork has shown the mythical tree as a ceiba tree. The Maya believed the gods planted ceibas for each of the directions—a white ceiba in the north, a black tree in the west, a red ceiba in the east, and a yellow one in the south.

THE CEIBA TREE

Ceiba trees, native to Mexico, Central America, the Caribbean, and South America, can grow over two hundred feet tall! The younger trees have a dark green trunk, symbolizing life and growth. The trees were sacred to the ancient Maya, and many are protected today. The ceiba is the national tree of Guatemala, where a four-hundred-year-old ceiba proudly stands.

FIND THESE WORDS RELATED TO MAYA MYTHOLOGY IN THE PUZZLE BELOW.

```
W V U N D E R W O R L D J X V
C O E G D Y T L A M Y Q M L P
O R H P O P O L V U H G N U H
R K K B O M S N L V H M N C D
N B D R A U E H M V U J W L Q
W G R Z F L O B B C N P Z I P
R A N Q Q U L E N E T B Z M O
W D H N T W G P P I E V M R G
Q A R D Y H Y I L B R N I X M
J F W C I C E X U A S L B C H
A T P L D O T R J K Y G X X O
E C Z A U D R L S P F E R G W
O H L Y H F I P C H S G R H O
O X W A H E R O T W I N S S O
D E S A H A M F E T Z E A T D
```

Hero Twins

Brothers

Ballplayers

Hunters

Corn

Clay

Wood

Ceiba

Underworld

Popol Vuh

WHO'S WHO IN THE ANCIENT MAYA WORLD

People only became rulers if they were born into a royal family or married into one. Kings and queens controlled their city-states but received help from advisors, priests, and astronomers. They oversaw the local water supply, traded valuable items with outside communities, and decided when to declare war against enemy city-states.

Rulers had to appear brave and powerful before their people. Some kings wore jaguar skins because they thought it made them look as fierce as the large jungle cats themselves. Maya royalty also wore feathered headdresses. The colorful feathers usually came from birds like the quetzal (say: KETZ-el) and the macaw. Only rulers, priests, or special warriors adorned themselves with the rare feathers and prized skins of these beautiful animals.

THE MAYA'S MOST FAMOUS ROYALS:

 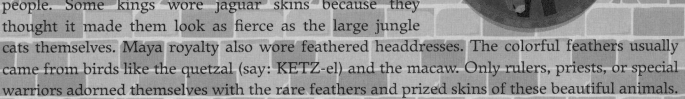

Lady Olnal was the first woman Maya ruler. She led the city of Palenque (in what is now the Chiapas state in Mexico) from 583 CE until her death in 604 CE.

Lady of Tikal was only six when she became queen of Tikal! (But she did have an adult advising her.)

King Pakal was the grandson of Lady Olnal. He took the throne in 615 CE, when he was only twelve! He was also known as Pakal the Great and Kinich Janaab Pakal. He ruled for sixty-eight years, the longest reign in Maya history. The lid of his tomb had a tree of life carved on it to signify how important King Pakal was.

Lady Six Sky ruled the city of Naranjo (in what is now Guatemala) from 682 until 741 CE, after her husband died. She led eight military victories and is sometimes pictured as a warrior king.

MAKE A MAYA HEADDRESS!

CREATE A HEADDRESS LIKE THE KIND WORN BY MAYA ROYALTY!

You will need:

- One sheet of construction paper
  (green will look most like quetzal feathers)
- Wide ribbon (at least 1 inch wide and about 3 feet long)
- Scissors
- Tape (clear tape or masking tape)
- Ruler
- Pencil

To get started:

1. Use the pencil to make a dot about 1 inch from the edge of the paper.
2. With the ruler, and using your dot as a guide, draw a line from the top to bottom of the page.
3. Fold along the line.
4. Turn the paper over.
5. Make more folds against the edge of your last fold, until you reach the end of the paper.
6. Use the scissors to cut along your 1-inch fold marks. You should have eight strips.
7. Cut all the strips in half to make sixteen shorter strips.
8. Cut the corners off of one end of each strip to form a point.
9. Tape the flat bottom of each strip to the ribbon. The strips should be close to one another.
10. Turn the ribbon over when you're through.
11. Hold the ribbon against your forehead and tie the ends behind your head, or ask someone to tie them for you.

THAT'S IT!
GREAT JOB, YOUR ROYAL HIGHNESS!

TO INVADE OR NOT TO INVADE? LET'S ASK VENUS!

Wars between city-states in the Maya world were quite common. Most wars were fought to gain control of trade routes. Royals also declared wars to show their strength and power. They wanted to earn and keep their citizens' respect. They also hoped to capture the warriors of their enemies and use them as sacrifices to the gods.

Weapons included spears, heavy sticks, swords, knives, axes, and in later years, bows and arrows. Warriors hid in the dense jungles to spy on their enemies. In addition to Lady Six Sky, other royal women may have fought in battles, too. For example, there are stelae that show Ix Naah Ek, a queen, wearing a warrior helmet and Lady K'abel holding a battle shield.

The Maya looked to the sky to learn many things. They thought the gods communicated with them through the movements of the stars and planets. Because the planet Venus shone so brightly, the Maya called it the night sun. They avoided war if Venus wasn't visible. But when Venus appeared, the Maya believed the gods approved of their battle plans.

All fighting stopped during the planting and gathering seasons. The Maya knew their lives depended on plentiful harvests, so wars were "off limits" during those times.

THE CASTLE

A stone pyramid that stands seventy-nine feet high—called El Castillo, or "The Castle"—was built in Chichén Itzá around the year 1000 CE to honor Kukulkan, also known as the Feathered Serpent God. There is a staircase on each of the pyramid's four sides.

Maya artists created sculptures of the heads of feathered snakes at the bottom of the northern stairway. A week before and after every equinox, a mix of light and shadow from the late-day sun casts an image of a feathered snake slithering down the pyramid!

The shadow that forms the snake's body appears to travel down the staircase as the sun changes position and meets one of the sculpture's large heads. Experts think the Maya used this twice-yearly event as a way to predict the arrival of the equinoxes and alert citizens to the approaching planting and harvesting seasons.

Later, the conquering Spanish placed a cannon on top of the large pyramid, which is perhaps why they thought of it as The Castle. What was once a temple became a symbol of the Spanish conquest.

THESE TEMPLES LOOK THE SAME BUT ARE NOT!

COMPARE THE TWO PICTURES. CAN YOU FIND SIX DIFFERENCES?

THE END OF AN ERA

Many city-states in the southern lowlands, including Palenque, Tikal, and Copán, collapsed between the years 800 and 1000 CE. Experts believe the cause may have been a lack of rainfall that caused a terrible drought. Clearing forests of their trees made the drought worse and ruined the soil. That led to a shortage of crops—and not enough food—for the overpopulated area. As a result, people fled north, perhaps convinced that the gods no longer favored their kings and queens.

Over time, power struggles led to many wars that weakened the Maya society.

When explorers from Spain landed in the region in the early 1500s, Spanish rulers decided to claim the territory. Soldiers arrived not long afterward. They carried smallpox and other diseases that quickly spread throughout the New World—the term then used to describe the Americas. A large part of the Maya population died as a result.

The conflict between the Maya and Spain's warriors began in 1524 in what is now western Guatemala. The Maya fought hard over the years, but they were outmatched by Spain's guns and horses. The last Maya city, the capital of the Itzá kingdom called Nojpeten, fell in 1697.

Nearly 150 years later, most people living outside Mesoamerica were unaware that the ancient Maya civilization ever existed. That changed when an American lawyer, John Lloyd Stephens, and a British artist, Frederick Catherwood, explored the area in 1839 and 1842. Two books written by Catherwood and Stephens included drawings of the pyramids, temples, and stelae buried in the jungles of Central America. Their work brought attention to the region and to the Maya culture.

STEPHENS AND CATHERWOOD

A LIVING CULTURE

When the Spanish arrived on the Yucatán Peninsula in the 1500s, they recorded thirty-one Mayan languages! The approximately six million Maya living in the region today still speak them. Many treasure their ancient past. They ask for help from their local shamans, who consult the ancient calendar and give advice. Women still weave cloth on looms. Men still weave palm leaves into roofs for their homes. They remember those who came before them and understand the need for keeping their traditions alive.

AN AMAZING MAYA MAZE

GRAB YOUR LANTERN AND EXPLORE THE UNDERGROUND TUNNELS TO FIND THE SECRET ENTRANCE TO AN ANCIENT MAYA TEMPLE!

ANSWER KEY

PAGE 7

PAGE 13

•••• + •••• = 8

•••• + •••• + ▬▬ = 18

$\overset{\bullet\bullet}{\underset{\equiv}{}}$ + •• = 19

$\overset{\bullet}{\equiv}$ − •••• = 2

•••• + ▬▬ + $\overset{\bullet\bullet\bullet\bullet}{\underline{\quad}}$ − ••• = 15

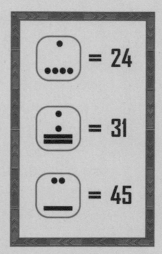

$\boxed{\overset{\bullet}{\underset{\bullet\bullet\bullet\bullet}{}}}$ = 24

$\boxed{\overset{\bullet}{\underset{\equiv}{}}}$ = 31

$\boxed{\overset{\bullet\bullet}{\underset{-}{}}}$ = 45

It was another beautiful day. The (water) was clear. The (sky) was blue.

A (crocodile) swam by slowly. He saw his friend the (turtle) reading a (book) in the grass nearby.

"Come on in," the (crocodile) called out. "The (water) feels great!"

"I'd love to!" said a (jaguar) from the edge of the riverbank.
He jumped in, splashing (water) all over the (turtle) and her (book).

"Looks like the (water) came to me!" she said.

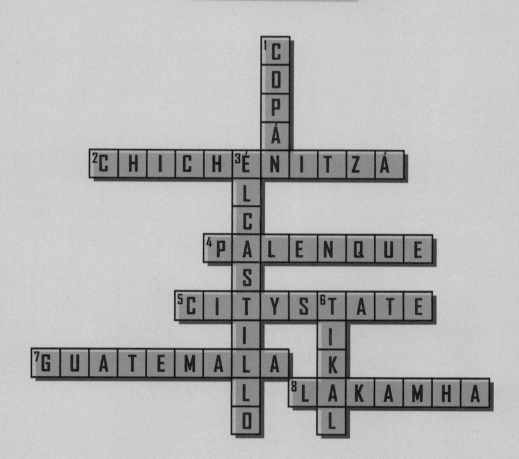

PAGE 23

```
W V U N D E R W O R L D J X V
C O E G D Y T L A M Y Q M L P
O R H P O P O L V U H G N U H
R K K B O M S N L V H M N C D
N B D R A U E H M V U J W L Q
W G R Z F L O B B C N P Z I P
R A N Q Q L E N E T B Z M O
W D H N T W G P P I E V M R G
Q A R D Y H Y I L B R N I X M
J F W C I C E X U A S L B C H
A T P L D O T R J K Y G X X Q
E C Z A U D R L S P F E R G W
D H L Y H F I P C H S G R H O
D X W A H E R O T W I N S S O
D E S A H A M F E T Z E A T O
```

PAGE 27

PAGE 29